LORD

KEEP

D1531712

SANE

365

INTRODUCTION

Peace where are you? My head hurt and I cannot think!

OMG seems like every time I take a step forward I end up falling back and I'm still in the same place. My mind is cluttered and my eyes are so sore from crying.

Have you ever felt this way? Are you about to just lose it and go crazy in your mind? In a world of chaos, it is hard

to keep a sane mind. So you are searching for normal but its running from you. Therefore, you cry out LORD KEEP ME SANE 365!

Index

CHAPTER 1
DEFINING THE MIND

CHAPTER 2
CHOICES

CHAPTER 3   **The**
cry out

CHAPTER 4
Shacking with a stranger

CHAPTER 5   **A**
sober mind

CHAPTER 6
Appreciating

CHAPTER 7
STAYING UNRUFFLED

CHAPTER 8   **A**
SECOND CHANCE

CHAPTER 9   **Be A U**
Beautiful

CHAPTER 10
POEMS

CHAPTER 1

Defining the mind

When I was a little girl I used to hear people pray this prayer: Lord keeps me in my right mind, Lord keep me sane. Back then I was an adolescent and didn't understand and my mind would wander; Are they going crazy? Now that I am an adult and I have been through somethings it's a testimony to say: life will toss you a curveball when you least expect it. It doesn't say ready or not here I come. Yet, in your juvenile years, you got mad at your parents and you made statements like "I can't wait till I'm grown." Then that eighteen birthday and graduation came and now you got it all to figure out in your head; no worries huh.

Everything was peachy at mom's house. Oh but now you're on your own, and things start to crumble. Therefore, you realize reality isn't like the movies. The storms of life are heavy and you're not bouncing back like you want to. One thing that we know that this is not a good place to be in life. Bills are piling up; kids keep asking for more. Let's talk about your mind, it is muddled and It is so hard to function. Just like a crowded room, it is hard to move around in it and so is your mind.

Before you go on reading ask yourself these three questions: be honest

1. What has your mind scattered at this moment?

2. Can the agendas on your mind wait or it has to be done right now?

3. Is it an option or a priority?

*Remember this: you can't eat an elephant at one time you have to break it down piece by piece. The elephant represents life: take it one day at a time.

Now take 3 deep breaths to inhale, exhale, inhale, exhale

Inhale, exhale.

Now say Lord keep me sane 365.

So at this time, you should be relaxing after that breathing exercise.

Know that you have the right to be sane.

What does it mean to be sane one might ask? The definition of sane is to have a healthy mind (brain): able to think normally.

There many different ways the brain can go, and we all want it to go in the right direction. The brain weights 3

Pounds, and it only represents two percent of our body weight. The human brain has one hundred billion brain cells and is an ever-changing organ. If someone has depression they can drop brain cells but if treated these cells can grow back. Therefore, if you are like me every little brain cell counts.

Chapter 2

Choices

We make good or bad choices in our minds. You can make a decision to have light or darkness; to die or survive on this journey

 In 1 Kings chapter 17 (KJV) staring at verse 8 ending at verse 16, there is a story

8 And the word of the LORD came unto him, saying,

9 Arise, get thee to Zarephath, which belongeth to Zidon, and dwell there: behold, I have

commanded a widow woman there to sustain thee.

¹⁰ So he arose and went to Zarephath. And when he came to the gate of the city, behold, the widow woman was there gathering of sticks: and he called to her, and said, Fetch me, I pray thee, a little water in a vessel, that I may drink.

¹¹ And as she was going to fetch it, he called to her, and said, Bring me, I pray thee, a morsel of bread in thine hand.

¹² And she said, As the LORD thy God liveth, I have not a cake, but an handful of meal in a barrel, and a little oil in a cruse: and, behold, I am gathering two sticks, that I may go in and dress it for me and my son, that we may eat it, and die.

¹³ And Elijah said unto her, Fear not; go and do as thou hast said: but make me thereof a little cake first, and bring it unto me, and after make for thee and for thy son.

¹⁴ For thus saith the LORD God of Israel, The barrel of meal shall not waste, neither shall the cruse of oil fail, until the day that the LORD sendeth rain upon the earth.

¹⁵ And she went and did according to the saying of Elijah: and she, and he, and her house, did eat many days.

¹⁶ And the barrel of meal wasted not, neither did the cruse of oil fail, according to the word of the LORD, which he spoke by Elijah.

In this passage, we find that this woman is in a dark place. Verse 9 states that she is a widow: once married but now her husband is deceased.

The widow of Zarephath is a single mother at this moment. Tell me if this sounds familiar; her baby

Daddy gone and now she is left to feed the child on her own. She is working to put a meal on the table. Oh, but it is something different about this meal she said this is her last meal before her and her child dies. Where is her mindset in this stage of her life?

Is this the right choice for her and her child? Let us remember that at this time: there were not any Department of Human

Services, (FYI) no food stamps or food banks that she could go get help from. Her mental state is in a dreary zone. The widow wanted to die and wanted her son to die.

It's one thing to want to give up the ghost but to take someone with you. The situation she was in was not very normal. What was the driving force behind her feeling this way?

In verse 13 Elijah let us know exactly what it was.

It was fear. Elijah told her fear not, Now the damsel has an alternative path to take: however, she has two choices worry or not to worry. Just like Elijah told her not to accept fear. God is telling you not to be overwhelmed because your life has changed direction. And 2 Timothy 1:7 states for God has not given us a spirit of fear, but of power and of love and of a sound mind.

For example; you made have had a nice home and a car but it got reposed. It is not the end of the world. You may have lost your job but keep your head up. In God's word, it tells us in Matthew 6: 19 do not lay up for yourselves treasures on earth, where moth and rust destroy and where thieves break in and steal; **20**but lay up for yourselves treasures in heaven, where neither moth nor rust destroys and where thieves do not break in and steal. **21**For where your treasure is, there your heart will be also.

Therefore, do not get bogged down with material things.

The second thing that Elijah told the damsel in verse 13 was to go and do what as thou has said. She decided to do what the Prophet had instructed her to do: and her life was changed. She went from a scrap of a meal to eat for many days. If we would just do as our Father in heaven has instructed us in his word; it would save us from a lot of suffering. The Lord almighty is there to help you in all situations, that means everything. It is your choice to accept him or deny his help. If you do not know him get to know him say the Sinners Prayer: and be saved.

Romans 10:9

That if thou shalt confess with thy mouth the Lord Jesus, and shalt believe in thine heart that God hath raised him from the dead, thou shalt be saved.

Chapter

3

The cry out

As we look further into this woman's

life, she made a preference; to live. The

widow's mind is healthy and she is not

starving. Here comes another difficult situation; 1 Kings 17;

¹⁷ And it came to pass after these things, that the son of the woman, the mistress of the house, fell sick; and his sickness was so sore, that there was no breath left in him.

¹⁸ And she said unto Elijah, What have I to do with thee, O thou man of God? art thou come unto me to call my sin to remembrance, and to slay my son?

¹⁹ And he said unto her, Give me thy son. And he took him out of her bosom and carried him up into a loft, where he abode and laid him upon his own bed.

²⁰ And he cried unto the LORD, and said, O LORD my God, hast thou also brought evil upon the

widow with whom I sojourn, by slaying her son?

²¹ And he stretched himself upon the child three times, and cried unto the LORD, and said,
O LORD my God, I pray thee, let this child's soul come into him again.

²² And the LORD heard the voice of Elijah; and the soul of the child came into him again, and he revived.

²³ And Elijah took the child, and brought him down out of the chamber into the house, and delivered him unto his mother: and Elijah said, See, thy son liveth.

²⁴ And the woman said to Elijah, Now by this I know that thou art a man of God, and that the

word of the LORD in thy mouth is truth.

Her child is sick and she wants him to live so she goes and takes him to the man that saved them from dying. Now she has a desire for her and the child to survive. The child is barely breathing. It's too much for her to take on so she seeks help. A lot of people are going insane because of their adult children or kid's problems. And It gets to be an abundance of worry that you cannot handle by yourself. When you get to this point seek out help

as the widow did for her child. She took her child to Elijah. On this journey call life if you seek some assistance that would take a lot of pressure off of you. And he took the child and cried out unto the Lord and prayed. This was a situation that Elijah could not handle by himself it was too much

he could not fix this, so he prayed.

In life, a lot of our friends or acquaintances put their troubles on us. Therefore, you have your pains and sorrows, and someone else's. That can be too much on one individual mindset.

Just remember that prayer has never failed anyone.

Don't be ashamed to cry out to the Lord. Psalms 116 and 1 (KJV)

I love the LORD because he hath heard my voice and my supplications.

There is a devotional song that we sing that says

I LOVE THE LORD HE HEARD MY CRY, AND PITTED MY EVERY GROAN; LONG AS I LIVE AND TROUBLE RISE I'LL HASTE UNTO HIS THRONE.

This is so true the Lord will help if u call on him.

The elders often have said I have a telephone in my Bosom and I can call on my Savior anytime.

When things get heavy on your mind and you about to lose it don't pull out your cell phone, access the phone in your bosom. Nothing is too big or to small that Jesus cannot handle. He can do everything but fail. Darkness will come in your life

and it will try to take over your mindset. Don't let it. You can walk with the light. Find your second wind, your inner strength. The definition of will power is the task to control oneself and determines one's action. Use your energy to move and in a positive manner.

Proverbs 18:21
Death and life are in the power of the tongue: **and** they that love it shall eat the fruit thereof.

Put this question to thought:

How do you want to be sane or insane?

Hopefully, you chose sane so speak it you have the potential to do it.

Chapter 4

Shacking with strangers

When I was a little girl growing up in the 70" s. One day I was at my Grandma Babe's house, she needed to use the phone. She asks me to see if anyone was on the line because they had party lines. I pick up the telephone and two women were talking. Grandma asks me if anyone was on the phone. Yes, "I said: they said she is shacking with that man". And the nosey side of me ask Grandma Babe what is shacking? "Living with someone you're not supposed to live with, people that live together and not married," grandma said. Some of us are shacking with strangers in our minds.

In Galatians 5 and 22 (KJV)

But **the** fruit **of the Spirit** is love, joy, peace, longsuffering, gentleness, goodness, faith, Meekness, temperance: against such **the**re is no law.

Therefore, if your mind is not on theses' things you are shacking with a stranger in your mind.

Let's talk about an Egyptian handmaid in the bible name Hagar in

Genesis 16 (KJV)

⁴ And he went in unto Hagar, and she conceived: and when she saw that she had conceived, her mistress was despised in her eyes.

Hagar was a young woman who got a slap in the face by life. One day she was minding her own business doing her job. And now her employer has forced his self on her and she is pregnant because of his wife's treacherous plan. The bible never said how she felt about Abraham, but she loathes Sarah.

A happy young lady full of love and joy is now mad with hatred and bitterness. So now she is shacking with a stranger. The bible said she despised her mistress and the word despised means hated.

When your mind goes to this hate stage you are shacking with a stranger.

God never intended for us to detest our brothers and sisters. To be in this state of mind will get you in serious trouble; because of her hatefulness toward Sarah. Sarah retaliated back: let us not forget that:

You reap what you sow: what you dish out if it is thrown back to you would you be able to handle it. Therefore, people that you talk hateful and sassy too if they did that to you how would that make you feel. Hmm, something to think about. Yes; so treat others how you want to be treated.

Genesis 16 (KJV)

[6] But Abram said unto Sarai, Behold, thy maid is in thine hand; do to her as it pleased thee. And when Sarai dealt hardly with her, she fled from her face. Definition of hardly means harshly.

How would you feel if you were Hagar? Could you still love?

Hatred caused Hagar's attitude to change for the worse. There are penalties for your actions good are bad. Sarah lashes back a Hagar for her attitude. Hagar left home. Hatred will make you do things that you will be shame of. One thing it will do is make you act before thinking. Yes, it will cause you to do a Bozo: un huh a clown, or make a fool out of yourself. She left her place of employment. Unfortunately, I have been this type of mad. Quitting a job before thinking. Now I can say to everyone don't leave your job unless u have another one to go to. Yes, we walk by faith: and the definition of faith is the substances of things hoped for and the evidence unseen. However, make sure you are consulting God in prayer before you make a hasty move like abandoning your job. Common sense lets us know that it takes substances to pay bills.

People or just one person may be making you stress on your job. But leaving your occupation and avoiding bill collectors is not a way to live. It will add more worry to your life. Consequently; this is not being in a sane mind when you are burden down.

Take note that in her resentment Hagar never cursed Sarai out. A lot of people don't know how to express their anger in words so instead of being silent they use bad language. And this causes situations to get heated very fast. Throwing ugly words at someone in a rage causes your heart rate to rise. This will cause a harmful toll on your health. And using the Lord's name in vain is a dangerous peal on your soul.

Exodus 20:7 King James Version
Thou shalt not take the name of the LORD thy God in vain; for the LORD will not hold him guiltless that taketh his name in vain.

Note that A potty mouth is not being very Christian. God is not pleased.

Also, you have created a tense work environment. Especially if you are the type of person that comes into work just cussing to be cussing. And then say yawl have to excuse me. If you make this statement you already know you were inappropriate. This type of worker is very unprofessional and doesn't care about other's feelings in the workplace. Now you racking your mind wondering why people don't want to eat lunch or leave the room when you enter. People who cuss a lot give off negative energy and usually are unhappy. Workforce hours are usually from 8 to 12 hours and can be stressful. People try to stay positive and drama free. Some people refrain from this kind of language. So be mindful of people's feelings.

So Sari deals with her hardly, and Hagar does not like this treatment. She flees. Have you ever left a job because someone made you mad? Maybe someone did something to you that wasn't fair.

Do not make choices in your annoyance. Hagar made a swift choice without thinking. She was shacking with hatred in her mind and could not think straight. But Hagar had a happy ending she had a guardian angel looking out for her. Lessons from Hagar life

We have acquired these teachings from her life

1. Not to make haste decisions

2. Treat others how you want to be treated

3. Watch our language

Chapter 5

A SOBER MIND

To have a sane awareness you must have a sober mind. The definition of sober is not to be affected by alcohol not drunk. A tipsy mind

can be a dangerous one. A lot of people think that

being intoxicated makes them forget their problems. Not true it adds to it. Especially

if it becomes a habit. And to be sober also means not to be in a chemically altered state where your judgment may be weakened. This chapter is not to condemn anyone for drinking, but to help them understand that it doesn't resolve difficulties. It is a proven fact that too much can have destructive results.

The first time wine was introduced in the bible was in the book of

Genesis chapter 9 verse 20&21

20 And Noah began to be a husbandman, and he planted a vineyard:

21 And he drank of the wine, and was drunken; and he was uncovered within his tent. (KJV)

So we see in this passage that Noah has consumed so much that he got out of his clothes and lay naked in the open. Yes, he was in his own home but it was not acceptable for this type of behavior.

Genesis 9 22-27

22 And Ham, the father of Canaan, saw the nakedness of his father, and told his two brethren without.

23 And Shem and Japheth took a garment, and laid it upon both their shoulders, and went backward, and covered the nakedness of their father; and their faces were backward, and they saw not their father's nakedness.

24 And Noah awoke from his wine, and knew what his younger son had done unto him.

²⁵ And he said, cursed be Canaan; a servant of servants shall he be unto his brethren.

²⁶ And he said, Blessed be the LORD God of Shem; and Canaan shall be his servant.

²⁷ God shall enlarge Japheth, and he shall dwell in the tents of Shem; and Canaan shall be his servant.

For a man to look upon another man's naked body was not suitable manners. Now let's analyze this

Noah had gotten drunk, pulled off his clothes, laid naked.

His son Ham came to visit and saw this. He runs and tells his two brothers that dad is drunk and I had seen him naked. So the brothers go in and cover Noah. He wakes up from a drunken state and founds out what has happened and gets mad at Ham and curse ham's son Canaan.

We have seen this type of behavior in real life and movies where people become drunk and strip out of their clothes. And they blame someone else for their actions or curse everyone out. For Noah it was recorded in the bible there were no pictures on snap chat, but in the year 2020, there are social media. Many young girls have gotten drunk at a party and strip down are doing something they wish to hide, but it is all over social media and their body parts exposed. This type of exposure has caused some people to commit suicide or try to end their lives. They need to know that it's not the end of the world. People do and can recover from this.

Maybe you are like me, and you know how people can become violent behind alcohol. I have never understood this type of behavior. You beat someone you supposedly love, and the next day you can't stand to look at their bruised face or try to hide them from their family because you have a drinking problem. Some people don't have drinking problems and do this type of abuse, they are mental. If you are the victim in either of these cases get help. No one has the right to bash in your face. This is not the 70's and 80's where

Women were taught to take it and keep silent.

Let's take another biblical character King Asaharius in the book of Esther where being drunk caused him to make an intoxicating decision that caused him to get a divorce.

Esther Chapter 1 verse 10-12

10 On the seventh day, when the heart of the king was merry with wine, he commanded Mehuman, Biztha, Harbona, Bigtha, and Abagtha, Zethar, and Carcas, the seven chamberlains that served in the presence of Ahasuerus the king,

11 To bring Vashti the queen before the king with the crown royal, to shew the people and the princes her beauty: for she was fair to look on.

12 But the queen Vashti refused to come at the king's commandment by his chamberlains: therefore, was the king very wroth, and his anger burned in him.

As you can see again liquor changes the state of mind, and your intoxicated actions affect the people around you. She did not want to be paraded around in front of a lot of drunken men.

So the Queen Vashti refused to come. Perhaps you can relate to the Queen. Some of us have that one drunk relative uncle, aunty, the cousin that wanted you to parade around and dance with them at the family functions. Question? Do these people realize how their breath usually smells like vomit? It seems that when people are in this state, they want to put their arm around you and breathe right in your face. Isn't that uncomfortable for you?

The Queen did not want to be around people like that, or else she would have come. Now we have melding people: If the King wasn't worried why should they

Esther Chapter 1 15-20

What shall we do unto the queen Vashti according to law, because she hath not performed the commandment of the king Ahasuerus by the chamberlains? 16 And Memucan answered before the king and the princes, Vashti the queen hath not done wrong to the king only, but also to all the princes, and to all the people that are in all the

provinces of the king
Ahasuerus.

17 For this deed of the queen
shall come abroad unto all
women, so that they shall
despise their husbands in their
eyes, when it shall be reported,
The king Ahasuerus
commanded Vashti the queen to
be brought in before him, but
she came not.

18 Likewise shall the ladies of
Persia and Media say this day
unto all the king's princes,
which have heard of the deed of
the queen. Thus shall there
arise too much contempt and
wrath.

19 If it please the king, let there
go a royal commandment from
him, and let it be written among
the laws of the Persians and the

Medes, that it be not altered, That Vashti come no more before king Ahasuerus; and let the king give her royal estate unto another that is better than she.

20 And when the king's decree which he shall make shall be published throughout all his empire, (for it is great,) all the wives shall give to their husbands honor, both to great and small.

Now the King Ahasuerus who is merry with wine

Is letting people influence his decisions that will affect his life. Whatever good or bad conclusions you make in your life it affects the people around you. Therefore, when you make a choice make sure your mind is sober. Pray and ask God to help you make the right sensible decision.

CHAPTER 6

APPRECIATING

The word appreciating comes from the root word appreciate. Which means: recognize the full worth of. A lot of us are losing our minds because we don't distinguish what we are worth. Know who you are and what you are treasured, everyone has value. You mean something to someone, so get it together. God can use you, let him come into your life. Don't worry about what or who is not in your lifecycle, that will make you go insane.

Everyone wants to be accepted by someone. If we get rejected by the one, we are trying to get acceptance from. We tend to think no one loves us, or our world has come to an end.

My husband and I have bought a new home. I have been telling him that I need some new bar stools. The ones I have, we had brought them over from the old house they were setting on the front deck. I bought them at a yard sale 16 years ago. We could not agree on some new bar stools, so I stop bringing up the subject. Every time I walk by them stools I would get mad because I wanted new ones. The new house I wanted new stuff. My husband had pneumonia and a heart attack he went into the hospital. Because of COVID-19, I was not allowed to go in and visit. While he was sick and not at home I was bored. Once again I was walking by those stools but this time I saw potential in them. If I put a little tender love and care into them (work) they will be nice. I went to Walmart and I got some stuff to sand and stain those chairs. Oh me I tell you I began to cry because I didn't appreciate what I already had in my possession. I wanted to put it back outside, throw them away. I didn't even identify the splendor that they had beyond the dirt past the years of wear and tear and neglect. The barstools were old not up to my new standards and I didn't want them around. For some odd reason that day I had seen that they still had a purpose. Life was still in them if I gave them some restoration. My eyes had overlooked them. Why was my heart yearning for them now? What made me see them as that sad child that no one wants to pick on their team? Did I feel sorry for them? Was I in my feelings because I was lonely and could not be at the hospital with my husband. Did I care for these bar stools as a substitute for my spouse? Whatever the reason that day I learn a valuable lesson from God. As I was sobbing I began to recite the serenity prayer

God, grant me the serenity to accept the things I cannot change,

Courage to accept the things I can and Wisdom to know the difference.

The definition of serenity is the state of being calm, peaceful, and untroubled. Who doesn't want tranquility?

I had made a big deal out of something that I did not need

because I already had it. I learn to take what God has blessed me with and be happy. That was a cherished lesson I absorb: neglect not the things I already have in my grasp. In Matthew 25 14-30

the parable of the talent Jesus is teaching a lesson

14 For the kingdom of heaven is as a man traveling into a far country, who called his own servants, and delivered unto them his goods.

15 And unto one he gave five talents, to another two, and to another one; to every man according to his several ability; and straightway took his journey.

16 Then he that had received the five talents went and traded with the same, and made them other five talents.

¹⁷ And likewise he that had received two, he also gained other two.

¹⁸ But he that had received one went and digged in the earth, and hid his lord's money.

¹⁹ After a long time the lord of those servants cometh, and reckoneth with them.

²⁰ And so he that had received five talents came and brought other five talents, saying, Lord, thou deliveredst unto me five talents: behold, I have gained beside them five talents more.

²¹ His lord said unto him, Well done, thou good and faithful servant: thou hast been faithful over a few things, I will make thee ruler over many things: enter thou into the joy of thy lord.

22 He also that had received two talents came and said, Lord, thou deliveredst unto me two talents: behold, I have gained two other talents beside them.

23 His lord said unto him, Well done, good and faithful servant; thou hast been faithful over a few things, I will make thee ruler over many things: enter thou into the joy of thy lord.

24 Then he which had received the one talent came and said, Lord, I knew thee that thou art an hard man, reaping where thou hast not sown, and gathering where thou hast not strawed:

25 And I was afraid, and went and hid thy talent in the earth: lo, there thou hast that is thine.

26 His lord answered and said unto him, Thou wicked and slothful servant, thou knewest that I reap where I sowed not, and gather where I have not strawed:

27 Thou oughtest therefore to have put my money to the exchangers, and then at my coming I should have received mine own with usury.

28 Take therefore the talent from him, and give it unto him which hath ten talents.

29 For unto every one that hath shall be given, and he shall have abundance: but from him that hath not shall be taken away even that which he hath.

It is safe to say the servant with one talent did not appreciate what he had. He was blessed with something and didn't even use it. Why one might ask? Look back in verse 25. Fear yes fear was the factor that was holding him back it was torturing his mind from doing better. God provides us with things to share with others not to hide, so we can be a witness for his kingdom. He expects us to take care of what he puts in our possession.

When the Lord blesses you with something it is not to worry you or for you to be a shame of it. The gift that God gives you is to promote you not to block you. A stepping stone, not a stumbling block.

In Matthew Chapter 25 verse 21 &23

His lord said unto him, Well done, thou good and faithful servant: thou hast been faithful over a few things, I will make thee ruler over many things: enter thou into the joy of thy lord. Because the servant with five talents and the servant with two talents used what they had they were blessed with more. Consequently, if the Lord gives you just a little, show your appreciation by taking that and making it work. It could be a test of your loyalty.

Don't get worried over lemons make lemonade, even it has sugar in it not all bitter. I could have missed a lot of headaches in life if I just cherished the little things that were handed to me. Ok: so you stressed about little things how can you handle something bigger. Let's breathe and take THE TIME TO WRITE DOWN THINGS YOU HAVE OVERLOOK

OR DON'T APPRECIATE (BE HONEST)

Are there any individuals on that list? (Yes or No)

In a world of chaos, people don't appreciate each other as they use too. If you have a family, try to spend time with them. They may get on your nerves or have hurt you but rise above that and let go of the past for your sanity. There are homeless folks who don't have any family and they wish that they had somebody in their bloodline. Love what you have in your life. Yes, you can strive for more: but don't forget to work with what you already have.

CHAPTER 7
STAYING UNRUFFLED

The definition of unruffled
: poised and serene especially
in the face of setbacks or
confusion.

During confusion or setbacks
can you stay unruffled, in other
words calm, level, unshaken,
and peaceful. The enemy's job
is to destroy your personality.
Now that you are aware of this;
now you can be prepared to
keep your charm. If the
adversary can pull you off your
character, he or she may also
try and pull you away from God.

Let's take a look at King David and how a person came to him trying to pull him out of his character in

2 Samuel 16

[5] And when king David came to Bahurim, behold, thence came out a man of the family of the house of Saul, whose name was Shimei, the son of Gera: he came forth, and cursed still as he came. [6] And he cast stones at David, and at all the servants of king David: and all the people and all the mighty men were on his right hand and on his left.

[7] And thus said Shimei when he cursed, come out, come out,

thou bloody man, and thou man of Belial:

Whoa! This would make the average person do some insane stuff. This would be a moment where I would have said lord keep me sane 365.   David and his men traveling minding their own business. Now here comes Shimei cussing King David. Shimei is trying to pick a fight with David and he calls David Belial which in Hebrew means devil. Maybe you can relate; you and your friends out minding your own business and someone thinks yall looking at them or talking about them. Now that person is cussing at you and your group or throwing things calling you out of your name.

Question? Can you keep your cool in this kind of situation? Will you be intimidated? The majority of the human race would be ruffled. The bible teaches us

In Ephesians 4 and 26 :

Be angry, and sin not.

I love the way King David handled the situation.

1 Samuel 16 verse 10-11

10 And the king said, What have I to do with you, ye sons of Zeruiah? so let him curse, because the LORD hath said unto him, Curse David. Who shall then say, Wherefore hast thou done so?

11 And David said to Abishai, and to all his servants, Behold, my son, which came forth of my bowels, seeketh my life: how much more now may this Benjamite do it? let him alone, and let him curse; for the LORD hath bidden him.

Shimei was not a match for David, and the king recognized that he had to be the bigger person. Yes, he could have had him killed, but he told his servants to leave him alone.

There will be times in life where the enemy will try to ruffle your feathers. Be smart don't display that you can be a bad actor. The best way to get back at an opponent is to act like they don't bother you. Turn on the ignore button. When they see that they cannot phase you, they will leave you alone. Some people are just looking for someone to argue or fight with.

But be like king David don't let it stop you on your journey. Stay unruffled.

Chapter 8
A SECOND CHANCE

Inspirational story

One day, an old man was walking along a beach that was littered with thousands of starfish that had been washed ashore by the high tide. As he walked he came upon a young boy who was eagerly throwing the starfish back into the ocean, one by one.

Puzzled, the man looked at the boy and asked what he was

doing. Without looking up from his task, the boy simply replied, "I'm saving these starfish, Sir".

The old man chuckled aloud, "Son, there are thousands of starfish and only one of you. What difference can you make?"

The boy picked up a starfish, gently tossed it into the water, and turning to the man, said, "I made a difference to that one!"

author, Loren Eiseley(born September 3, 1907, Lincoln, NE died July 9, 1977, Philadelphia, PA)

The first point I want to make from this inspiring story is that never listen to the nay Sayers. God has never looked down on us for helping our neighbor. The golden rule ;

Is do unto others as you would have them do unto you.

The young boy in the story said he made a difference because it mattered to the one that got thrown back in. But what he was doing; was giving them a second chance. The starfish was lying on the beach drying out, lifeless. Thinking that no one cared and waiting to die. Tossed back into the ocean by the little boy it has become saturated. It now has another chance to survive to make it, start over. Do you feel like a starfish that's been washed up on the shore waiting for someone to notice and help you? Don't give up dry your tears God is just like that little boy he will pick you up and throw you back in. He gives us chance after chance. He is an awesome wonder. Jesus told the woman at the well in water that you will never thirst again. Get wet in Christ. He is water in dry places. I dare you to be like this little boy. Give somebody another chance. Who have you ruled out of your life like the old man in the story? LAUGHING! Thinking their not gonna make it. But GOD! Remember that our lives are not ours but they belong to GOD. It doesn't matter where you are in your life God will reach down pick you up dust the dirt, fix the brokenness, heal the hurt, and love you right where you are. There was a song I used to sing when I was a young girl: Please be patient with me GOD is not through with me yet: but when GOD gets through with me I shall come forth as pure gold. You may be down but long as GOD wakes you in the morning you got another chance to start over to get it right to renew, restore, regroup, do better, and reinvent your life. YES! Tell depression, sadness, and darkness you're not welcome here. OH YEAH! HELP ME SAY: Lord keep me sane 365.

CHAPTER 9

BE A U BEAUTIFUL

When you look in the mirror what do you see? Do you love it are like it? how do you see yourself? Describe yourself? example: mother, father worker, etc.

_____

_____

_____

_____

_____

_____

_____

_____

_____

_____

_____

_____

_____

_____

_____

_____

_____

_____

_____

_____

_____

_____

_____

_____

_____

Beautiful should have been one
of the words to describe
yourself why you ask? In
Ecclesiastes 3:11 "He has
made everything beautiful in his

time."(KJV) Let's take the word everything definition:

1. all things; all the things of a group or class.2.

the current situation; life in general.

Therefore, everything includes you.

now let us look at the word beautiful, definition: pleasing the senses or mind

Beauty is in the eye of the beholder. How you see yourself is how others will perceive you.

When we spell the word Beautiful the first two letters are B-E:

BE that means exist yes you are a living breathing God made

creature(human being) Psalm 139:13-14 King James Version (KJV)

13 For thou hast possessed my reins: thou hast covered me in my mother's womb.

14 I will praise thee; for I am fearfully and wonderfully made: marvellous are thy works; and that my soul knoweth right well.

The next letter in beautiful is U. So I SAY TO U

BE U only you can be you, so what if you have a different view, style, or dreams. It is ok. Embrace that you are what God created. Your scars, tears, hardship, bruises, ups, downs, and mistakes have molded you into the person you are.

Isaiah 61:1-3

61 The Spirit of the Lord God is upon me; because the Lord hath anointed me to preach good tidings unto the meek; he hath sent me to bind up the brokenhearted, to proclaim liberty to the captives, and the opening of the prison to them that are bound;

2 To proclaim the acceptable year of the Lord, and the day of vengeance of our God; to comfort all that mourn;

3 To appoint unto them that mourn in Zion, to give unto them beauty for ashes, the oil of joy for mourning, the garment of praise for the spirit of heaviness; that they might be called trees of righteousness, the planting of the Lord, that he might be glorified.

Beauty for ashes: whatever you been through God got a beauty for you.

For the pain, you have experience in your life God has beauty for you.

You have survived it and it didn't kill you. Oh no it made you stronger, and wiser so I say to you:

Be alluring and appealing

Be charming and cute

Be dazzling and delightful

Be elite and exquisite

Be fascinating and fine

Be graceful and grand

Be life and love

Be magnificent and marvelous

Be Pleasing and pretty

Be splendid and stunning

Be fair and foxy

Be radiant and ravishing

Be A U Beautiful

but most of all

Be Sane 365

Jude 24-25 King James Version (KJV)

24 Now unto him that is able to keep you from falling, and to present you faultless before the presence of his glory with exceeding joy,

25 To the only wise God our Saviour, be glory and majesty, dominion and power, both now and ever.

LORD KEEP ME SANE 365

AMEN

CHAPTER 10 POEMS

1. I AM WHAT I SPEAK

2. SHACKING WITH STRANGERS

3. LORD KEEP ME SANE 365

I am what I speak

I am what I speak from my
head to my feet

when I rise up for the day I
speak positive things my way

I am what I talk and the joy of
the Lord is in my walk

A beautiful child of Zion, an heir to the throne

my heart filled with peace my mouth is filled with songs,

Ahh! please listen as I speak these words in the air

The Lord is your shepherd your burdens he bears

You are what you Speak, from your head to your feet

When you rise up for the day speak positive things your way

To bless to be Stress, to Anointed to be disappointed

Children of God please speak this way

author

Minister Tammy Bray-Wright

Shacking with a Stranger

Shacking with a Stranger had my soul in danger

See I was shacking with MR HATE

he kept pulling and pulling: pulling all he could take

shacking with a stranger had my soul in danger

as I set up in my bed I started reminiscing in my head

I got up and put my feet on the floor

I said MR HATE pack your bags and go

shacking with a stranger had my soul in danger

He looked at me with a silly little grin

he said little Ms. Muffit you let in

shacking with a stranger had my soul in danger

I said MR HATE I'll make this simple

this right here is Jesus Christ Temple

Oh he got mad and did he flee he seen

the Holy Spirit that abided in me

See I got my joy back

I got my peace Back

and most of all I got my sleep back

ok, my friend, I want to tell you this

please be careful and put this on your list

 be aware of MR. Hate that slick foot stranger

so you want shack and have your soul in danger

author

Minister Tammy Bray-Wright

Lord keep Me Sane 3-6-5

Lord keep Me sane 3-6-5

as I deal with all these folks and their jive

Things with my I eyes that I do see

I beg for the world with one great plea

Lord Keep Me Sane 3-6-5

As I travel down this journey

seeking a way to survive

when I'm on my knees I do pray

Asking for your guardian angels to come my way

In my head, there is a fight

to do what is wrong or to do what is right

Lord keep me sane and in my right mind

as I go day by day and through the test of time

As I live and as I strive

Lord keep me Sane 3-6-5

author

Minister Tammy Bray-Wright

Scripture page

I Kings Chapter 17 8-24

Romans Chapter 10 Verse 9

Psalms Chapter 116 Verse 1

Proverbs Chapter 18 Verse 21

Galatians Chapter 5 Verse 22

Genesis Chapter 9   20-27

Exodus Chapter 20 Verse 7

Esther Chapter 1 10-20

Matthew Chapter 25 14-30

2 Samuel 16 5-11

Psalms 139 13-14

Ecclesiastes 3 Verse 11

Isaiah 16 1-3

Jude 24-25

Acknowledgements

I give God the glory for giving me the strength.

To my husband Marshall Wright thank you for being an awesome husband. You are truly the love of my life. Team Wright forever

To my children Lakeisha Ware – Butler and Ellery Elvon Ware

I love yawl to the moon and back. I'm very proud to have hard working children. I pray that this book will help you.

To my parents Cecil and Linda Bray

Thank you for teaching me how to have a house love. I thank God for blessing me with awesome parents.

To my granddaughters Iris and Dahlia

You will always have this book to lead and guide you. Trust God in everything you do.

To my two biological sisters Sandra Cooper and Sybrina Smith. Thanks for being there

for me down through the years.
If I don't have no one else in
the world I got my sisters.

Kisses

To my adopted siblings:
Kaylynn, Draven, Destiny and
Gabriel: I'm so proud to be your
big sister. Keep them good
grades coming.

To my two best friends Felisha
Morris and Rhonda Ramsey:
Thank you for loving me
through all my peculiar ways,
and for being that listening ear
when I need it.

To Sister Mary Blandon and
Mother Juanita Burris

Thank you for supporting my ministry since day one.

To my Pushmataha Lab team

Paulette, Jessah, Tommie, Kimberly, Bella, Zeth, Frances, Nicole, Gemma and Misty. Thank you for loving me. You Guys Rock! And to Paulette Schmidt thank you for being a Guru in the lab.

To the best church this side of heaven

Faith Assembly of God of Idabel, Ok

Thank you for accepting me and letting me preach.

I am forever grateful.

A special thanks to these organizations they have a special place in my heart:

Deborah Ministries Founder Dr. Vera Smith

Sister to Sister of Encouragement Founder Minister Tracy Williams

Christian Women Fellowship Founder

 Author Ann Bray Smith

Initiative for Marketing Success Alliance Team

Founder Author Ann Bray Smith

Artist spotlight:

Karenthia Calvin

Thank you for drawing my cover

Made in the USA
Columbia, SC
07 May 2022

59952462R00059